Abraham's Bright Beginning

Aspen R. Mcleod

Copyright © 2024

All rights reserved. No part of this publication may be reproduced, stored in a retrieval system or transmitted, in any form by any means without the prior consent of the author, nor be otherwise circulated in any form of binding or cover other than that with which it is published and without a similar condition being imposed on the subsequent purchaser.

ISBN: 978-0-578-27831-5

Dedicated to the Most High God of Israel and to whomever He sends this book to"

Love Aspen

The night Abram, the son of Terah was born it was known right away he had a huge purpose. King Nimrod was ruler at the time. His wise men studied the stars and saw a very large star from the heavens swallow four other stars and they were greatly amazed. The wise men knew this was a sign of a prophecy of what would take place soon. Baby Abram would grow to produce a huge nation that would conquer great kings and rule over many lands. The wise men shared the prophecy with Nimrod and this greatly troubled the King.

The King Ordered Terah to bring him his new son. He vowed to kill the baby to stop the prophecy from coming true. But Terah was excited over the birth ofbram and decided to bring a different child in Abram's place. The king took the child and he was never seen again. Meanwhile Terah took his son and his wife and hid them safely in a cave. Soon after, Abram and the prophecy were forgotten.

While in the cave, God was with Abram and he knew the Lord from 3 years old.

At the age of ten Abram was sent to his elders Noah and Noah's son Shem. They taught Abram the ways of the Lord. Thirty-nine years went by and Abram learned that his father Terah along with Nimrod worshipped idols made from wood and stone.

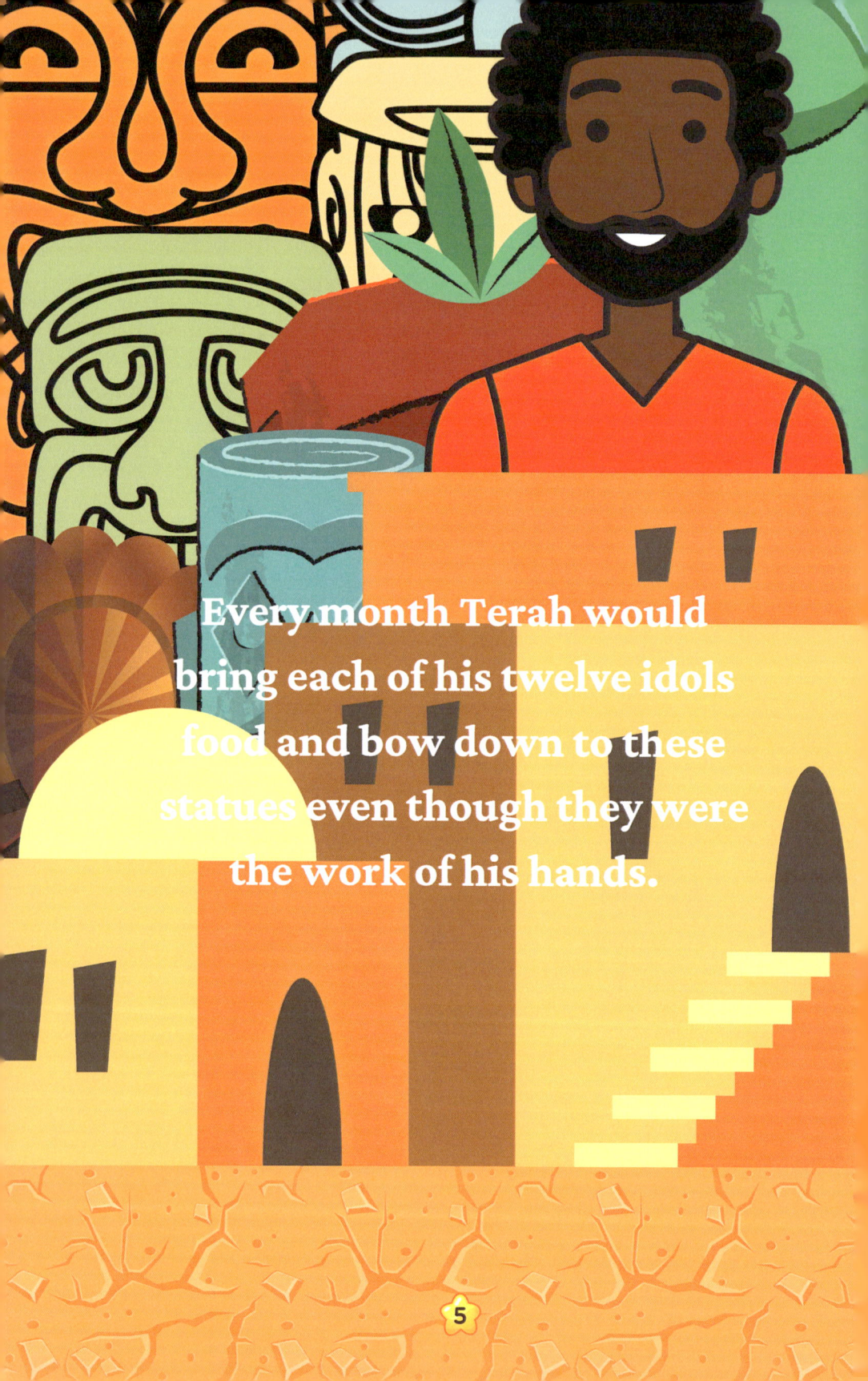

Every month Terah would bring each of his twelve idols food and bow down to these statues even though they were the work of his hands.

Abram left his father to ask his mother to cook meat for the statues. Abram watched as the idols did not reach out their hands to accept or eat the food. He thought to himself, maybe they did not like the food his mother prepared. The next day he brought better meat for the idols than before. Just as they did with the first meal, they did not move. In fact they did not eat, nor drink, or say "Thank you!"

Abram became very upset with his father. He grabbed a hatchet and began breaking all of his father's idols. Terah heard all of the commotion and ran in to see what was the matter. He found all of his idols smashed except the largest one. Terah angrily asked Abram what happened to his gods and Abram told him the largest smashed the others. Terah replied that the statue could not do this because he made it with his human hands.

"If this is so, why would you worship statues made with your own hands and not the god of our forefathers?"

Terah stormed out in a rage and went straight to Nimrod to tell him what Abram had done. Haran did not tell Terah to hide Abram, but in fear Terah lied to the king. Nimrod promised to kill Terah unless he brought both of his sons and Terah did so.

"Where did this son come from?"

"My eldest son Haran told me to deceive you and I did out of fear"

Haran was on Abram's side but he was not brave enough to go against the king. He said to himself whoever wins between his brother and Nimrod would be the side of his choice. Haran's mistake of not choosing the side of Abram not only showed he was lukewarm but this would later determine his fate.

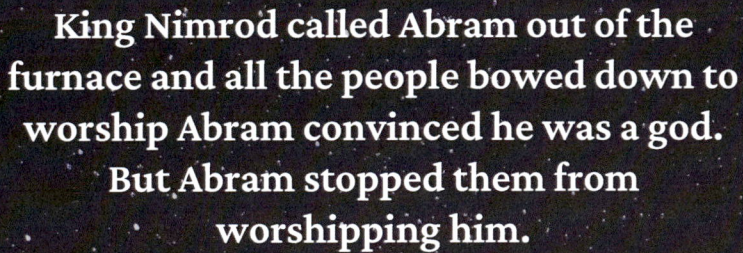

King Nimrod ordered all the gods made of wood and stone be thrown in the furnace. Even though Nimrod witnessed all of the miracles of the Most High with his own eyes, eventually he returned to his idols.

"I will only worship Abram's god. His god is the only true creator!"